NATIONAL GEOGRAPHIC

School Publishing

PIONEER EDITION

By Rebecca L. Johnson

CONTENTS

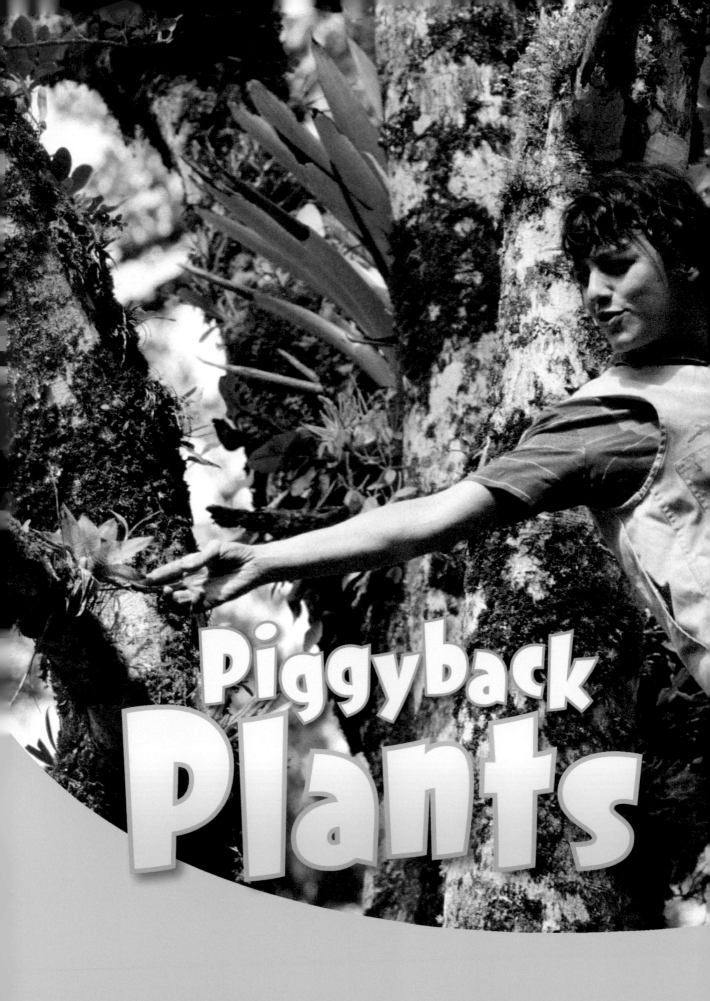

Piggyback Plants

Scientist Nalini Nadkarni hangs high above the ground. The tops of rainforest trees surround her. Small plants crowd the tree branches. What kind of plants live way up here?

Amazing Air Plants

The plants on the tree branches are **epiphytes** (ep-uh-FYTS). Epiphytes live on other plants. They grow piggyback, or on top of, them. People sometimes call epiphytes "air plants."

Dr. Nadkarni is an epiphyte expert. She studies epiphytes in rainforests. Epiphytes grow in other places, too. About 30,000 different kinds live on Earth.

Getting What's Needed

All plants need water and **nutrients**. How do epiphytes get these things? They get water from the air. They soak up raindrops, dew, and fog. Epiphytes get nutrients from dust in rainwater. They also get nutrients from dead leaves. The leaves get caught in epiphytes. The leaves turn into nutrients as they rot.

Up High. These types of epiphytes grow in Florida and the tropics.

Sunny and Safe

Epiphytes have a hard time when it's dry. Water and nutrients are harder to get. But epiphytes get lots of sunlight. They get more sunlight than plants on the forest floor.

Tree branches give epiphytes lots of space to grow. Epiphytes are less likely to be eaten than plants on the ground. Why? Few plant-eating animals live in the treetops.

Tagging Along. This rainforest tree has epiphytes living on it.

Flowers, Seeds, and Spores

Many epiphytes have big flowers. Birds, bees, and bats spread **pollen** from flower to flower. Flowers make seeds with pollen.

Some epiphytes don't have flowers. They make **spores** instead of seeds. Spores are like seeds, but are smaller and less complex.

Epiphytes make lots of seeds and spores. Most fall to the ground. But some land on branches where they **germinate**, or start growing.

Hanging On. This orchid cactus flower is a type of cactus. It is also an epiphyte.

5

Meet the Epiphytes

Let's meet some epiphytes.
Here are five well-known types.

Mosses

Ferns

Mosses have very small, simple bodies. Mosses make spores. The spores form on top of the plants. They look like fuzzy green fur.

Many epiphytes in rainforests are ferns. Ferns produce spores. Spores form in patches on fern leaves. Wind moves spores around. A few spores will land on trees. Here these spores can germinate and grow.

Bromeliads

Bromeliads (broh-MEE-lee-adz) have thick, tough leaves. The leaves grow in a circle around the plant's middle. Bromeliad flowers are showy. They have red, orange, pink, or yellow parts. Most of these parts are special leaves. The real flowers grow between them.

Orchids

Orchids (OR-kuhdz) have thick, waxy flowers. The flowers come in many colors. Some have spots or stripes. Orchid flowers make the world's smallest seeds.

Strangler Figs

Strangler figs are epiphytes with long roots. The roots grow down and around the tree trunk. The roots get bigger and bigger. They slowly squeeze, or strangle, the tree. Eventually the tree dies. Only the strangler fig is left.

These are a few of the best-known epiphytes. In fact, you've probably seen some of these yourself!

Wordwise

epiphyte: a plant that lives on another plant for support

germinate: when a seed starts to grow

nutrients: substances an organism needs to live and grow

pollen: dustlike particles that flowers need to make seeds

spore: a tiny structure made by nonflowering plants that can grow into a new plant

Treetop Ponds

Bromeliads have a special purpose in the rainforest. The leaves of some bromeliads form a cup, or tank. This tank is in the plant's middle. The tank fills with water when it rains. Some tanks are small. A large one might hold 18.9 liters (5 gallons) of water!

The bromeliad uses the water from its tank. Rainforest animals use the water, too. Insects lay eggs in it. Birds bathe in it. Monkeys use the tanks as drinking fountains.

Animal droppings fall into the tanks. Dead leaves do, too. These things put nutrients into the water. Bromeliad leaves soak these nutrients up.

Personal Pond. The water in this tank bromeliad forms a tiny pond.

A Soggy Home

Strawberry poison dart frogs also use bromeliad tanks. They use the tanks for their babies. The mother frog lays eggs on the ground. Tiny tadpoles hatch from them. The tadpoles get onto their mother's back. Then she climbs a tree. She puts each tadpole in a bromeliad tank. Each tadpole has its own private pond.

The mother frog feeds the tadpoles. How? She puts special eggs in the tanks. The tadpoles eat the eggs. The tadpoles become frogs. They climb out of their bromeliad ponds. They begin life on land.

Bromeliads are used in many ways by rainforest animals. Without them, some animals would not be able to survive.

Easy Access. The tadpole eats these special eggs in the tank.

tadpole

Hop On. The tadpole blends in with his mother as he rides on her back.

Piggyback Plants

Here's your chance to show what you know about epiphytes and how they live.

1 What are epiphytes?

2 How do epiphytes get water high above the ground?

3 Why do epiphytes make a lot of seeds or spores?

4 Name two different kinds of epiphytes. How are they different?

5 Why are tank bromeliads important to strawberry poison dart frogs?